KIM LEWIS

Building and Leading Teams

The New Supervisor's Guide to Nurturing Collaboration and Achieving Excellence

First edition

This book was professionally typeset on Reedsy.
Find out more at reedsy.com

Contents

1

Introduction

If you are a new supervisor, congratulations! My name is Kim Lewis, and I am a nursing supervisor at a correctional institution. Yes, I work with inmates. More importantly, I work with nurses, coaching them, advocating for them, and hopefully inspiring them to be their best selves. This may shock you, but I love what I do, and I am passionate about leading nurses. I am here to tell you that the anxiety that you are feeling is normal. I felt every bit of the imposter when I was promoted, to the point I had challenges signing my name with my new title.

You may have been in complete command in your previous role, but now you have a team of people looking to you to be the "boss". Your staff have different work ethics, different experience, different backgrounds and education. Pre-supervisory days, when you were struggling at work, you could just work harder, longer, and get the job done. Now you have to get the staff to pull together and achieve your goals.

This can be a very daunting idea for high achievers. Set aside the feelings that you are having that you can do this all yourself, that you can achieve the goals despite the cooperation of your team. If you could do it all by yourself, you wouldn't need to supervise the team, you would just do the work.

Holy crap! What have you done?!

Take a breath, take another. Now it may not always be easy, but you will get the hang of this supervisory thing. There are lots of books on leadership available to you, but this is just a short book that is designed to help you have early success as a new supervisor. This is not going to be the last book you are going to read on the topic. You clearly want to be good at what you do, that trait will carry you far, but carry that growth mindset forward and keep building your knowledge and skills.

2

Us vs Them

T he "Us vs. Them" mentality can be a significant hurdle to organizational success. This divisive mindset, where employees view themselves as distinct groups with conflicting interests, can undermine collaboration, innovation, and overall productivity.

Understanding Us vs. Them Mentality:

The Us vs. Them mentality often stems from various sources, including hierarchical structures, lack of communication, and competition for limited resources. Within organizations, it can manifest between departments, teams, or even individuals, hindering the flow of ideas and impeding progress.

The challenge of the new supervisor, especially one that is promoted from within the same organization, is that you may identify with the rank and file staff "us" and don't feel confident in the supervisory staff "us".

Us vs Them may not destroy an organization, it can make it significantly more dysfunctional and inefficient.

Reduced Collaboration: When teams view each other as competitors rather than collaborators, the exchange of ideas diminishes, hindering innovation and problem-solving.

Poor Communication: Departments operating in silos may experience breakdowns in communication, leading to misunderstandings, duplication of efforts, and missed opportunities.

Decreased Morale: The divisive nature of Us vs. Them thinking can create a negative work culture, resulting in lower morale, higher turnover rates, and increased stress among employees.

Innovation Stagnation: Cross-functional collaboration is often a catalyst for innovation. In an environment dominated by Us vs. Them thinking, the flow of creative ideas is stifled, impeding the organization's ability to adapt to change.

Strategies to Overcome Us vs. Them Mentality:

Promote Open Communication:

- Foster an environment where communication flows freely between departments and teams.
- Encourage regular meetings, cross-functional workshops, and collaborative projects to break down communication barriers.

Shared Goals and Values:

- Establish common organizational goals and values that transcend departmental boundaries.
- Emphasize the shared mission and vision to create a sense of unity and purpose

Leadership Role Modeling:

- Leadership should exemplify collaborative behavior, demonstrating unity across departments.
- Recognize and reward collaborative efforts to reinforce the importance of teamwork.

Cross-Training and Skill Sharing:

- Implement cross-training programs to enhance employees' understanding of different roles and functions within the organization.
- Facilitate skill-sharing initiatives to encourage the exchange of expertise among teams.

Celebrate Diversity:

- Embrace diversity and inclusion initiatives to build a more accepting workplace. Diversity can be your organizational super power if you lean into the ideas that can come from people of varying backgrounds.
- Highlight the strengths that each team member brings to the organization.

3

Building A Team

A high-performing team is a crucial asset for any organization, driving innovation, productivity, and overall success. As fun as team-building exercises can be, that isn't what we are talking about here (although that can be a component of building a team)

Define Clear Objectives:

Clearly articulate the team's purpose, goals, and objectives. Ensure that each team member understands their role in achieving these objectives.

SMART goals:

Specific: Goals are clearly articulated, avoiding vague or ambiguous language. "We will do five appointments daily to manage high-risk patients" is an example of a specific goal.

Whereas "we will see more patients" is very vague, does that mean one more patient or ten more patients.

Measurable: Establish measurable criteria to evaluate progress and success. Using these quantifiable metrics to track performance can also give teams a sense of accomplishment. It can also track performance and provide insight into the needs of the team.

Achievability: Objectives should be realistic and attainable within in a given timeframe. For example, referring back to the five high-risk patients per day, may not be sustainable long-term, but may be something that helps the team achieve specific goals.

Relevance: Ensure that objectives align with broader goals and achieve the overall mission. This can be especially challenging in large organizations with many layers of leadership. Never lose sight of the metrics that stakeholders value.

Time Bound: Set a timeframe for achieving objectives. That sense of urgency is essential for success. It provides a timeline for actions, and can ultimately establish a path for sustainability. Once you figure out how to climb the mountain, you have established the pathway to success.

Effective Communication:

Establish open lines of communication within the team. Just a reminder, an "open-door" policy should be you coming out the door to talk with your staff, not them coming into your office.

Your visibility makes a difference.

Encourage transparent and honest communication to foster trust and collaboration.

Set Expectations:

- Clearly define roles and responsibilities to avoid confusion. This does not mean putting people in silos where they only do one thing. However, there should be accountability for specific tasks within the team.
- Establish performance expectations and key performance indicators (KPIs) for each team member.

Build a Positive Team Culture:

- Foster a positive and inclusive team culture that encourages collaboration and mutual respect.
- Celebrate achievements and recognize individual contributions.

Provide Resources and Training:

- Ensure that the team has the necessary resources, tools, and training to perform their tasks effectively.
- Invest in continuous learning and development opportunities for team members.

Promote Team Bonding:

- Organize team-building activities to strengthen relationships and build trust.
- Foster a sense of camaraderie through shared experiences.

Effective Leadership:

- Lead by example and demonstrate the values and behaviors expected from the team.
- Provide guidance and support while empowering team members to take ownership of their work.

Encourage Innovation:

- Create an environment that values creativity and innovation.
- Encourage team members to share ideas and provide a platform for brainstorming and problem-solving.

Address Conflict Promptly:

- Recognize that conflict may arise and address it promptly and constructively.
- Encourage open dialogue to resolve issues and promote a healthy work environment.

Feedback and Recognition:

- Provide regular feedback to help team members improve and grow.
- Recognize and reward individual and team achievements.

Adaptability:

- Foster adaptability to navigate changes in the workplace.
- Encourage a mindset of continuous improvement and flexibility.

Measure and Evaluate Performance:

- Implement regular performance evaluations to assess individual and team progress.
- Use metrics and key performance indicators to track success and identify areas for improvement.

Celebrate Diversity:

- Embrace diversity within the team, recognizing that different perspectives contribute to innovation and problem-solving.

Encourage Work-Life Balance:

- Promote a healthy work-life balance to prevent burnout and maintain team morale.

Additionally, if you are involved with the hiring process, recruitment and selection can be a critical piece of developing the best possible team. How you mentor new staff can also impact retention.

4

From Me to We

In the business world where the competition is for sales and production, a "Me" mindset has been pervasive.

Michael Jordan is considered by many to be the greatest basketball player of all time, had a coach tell him, "There is no "i" in team." Jordan's reported response was, "There is no "i" in team, but there is an "i" in win." As great as Jordan was as a player, he did not win a championship until he got an additional star player (and future Hall of Famer) Scottie Pippen, thus demonstrating the power of "we". Michael Jordan's stature or status was not diminished by the addition of great players around him, but together they achieved greater success..

Many jobs require team efforts, just like basketball. Superstars help, but teamwork can cultivate a winning formula. Good effort from a good team and you get the shift from an individualistic "Me" mindset to a collaborative "We" culture. The "we" culture is becoming increasingly vital for organizational success. Embracing teamwork and fostering a collective spirit among employees not only enhances productivity but also promotes innovation and a positive work environment. By transitioning from "Me" to "We" in the workplace and building a collaborative culture we can increase job satisfaction in environments that lack extrinsic rewards.

The "Me" mindset is characterized by individual goals, achievements, and a focus on personal success. While individual contributions are valuable, an exclusive emphasis on personal gains can hinder overall team performance and organizational success. It can also be characterized by an unwillingness to help others.

Moving to "We"

Recognize the Power of Collaboration:
Collaboration brings together diverse perspectives, skills, and experiences to solve complex problems and drive innovation. Breaking down silos between departments, taking an interdisciplinary approach can be critical especially in large organizations.

Building Trust and Communication:
Trust is the foundation of a collaborative workplace. Encourage open communication, active listening, and transparency to create an environment where team members feel comfortable sharing ideas, expressing concerns, and working together towards common goals.

Shared Goals and Vision:
Aligning individual goals with the overarching vision and mission of the organization creates a sense of purpose and

unity. Clearly communicate the collective goals that the team is working towards, fostering a shared sense of responsibility and achievement. Having accountability within the team to accomplish goals brings the team together.

Learning from Setbacks and Measuring Collective Success:

In a collaborative environment, setbacks are viewed as learning opportunities for the team as a whole. Encourage a growth mindset that values resilience and continuous improvement, turning challenges into stepping stones for success. Shift the focus from individual achievements to collective success. Implement performance metrics that reflect team accomplishments and contributions to the organization's overall goals.

The leader of the team plays a vital role in facilitating the transition from "me" to "we". The leader has to lead by example. Recognizing the efforts of the team, rewarding collaborative success and accomplishments. You, as the leader, have to set the tone. Show up. Be visible. Communicate. Listen. Be open to ideas. And listen some more. There are no bad teams, only bad leaders. Start with listening to your team.

Embracing a "We" culture is not just a strategic choice; it is a powerful catalyst for sustained growth and excellence in today's interconnected and dynamic work environment.

A word of caution, not everyone will embrace a "we" culture. There are people that have zero regard for anyone unless it serves them. They lack empathy for the plight of others, they lack a sense of fairness unless they think what you are doing is unfair to them. They are impervious to "peer pressure" because they seemingly only care about the person they see in the mirror. The only thing this person will bring to the food share is their appetite. It is challenging to work with this personality. Minimize contact if they are a peer. If you supervise them, set forth very clear expectations and hold them accountable. Expect a lot of push back and argument.

5

Developing a Winning Culture

While the pursuit of success may seem synonymous with the corporate world, government and non-profit agencies are not exempt from the need for a winning culture. Establishing a culture of excellence in these sectors is crucial for delivering impactful services, fostering innovation, and maintaining public trust.

Define a Clear Mission and Values:

Clearly articulate the mission and values of the agency. This serves as the foundation for a shared sense of purpose and guides decision-making at all levels.

Transparent Communication:

Establish open lines of communication to keep employees informed about the agency's goals, strategies, and performance. Transparency builds trust and empowers staff to understand their roles in achieving the agency's mission.

Emphasize Public Service:

Instill a sense of pride and purpose in public service. Reinforce the impact of the agency's work on the community or the public it serves. Connecting employees to the larger societal goals enhances motivation and commitment.

Recognition of Public Servants:

Regularly acknowledge and celebrate the efforts of public servants. Recognition programs that highlight the positive impact of individual and team contributions help boost morale and reinforce the values of a winning culture.

Foster Collaboration Across Departments:

In government and non-profit agencies, collaboration is key to addressing complex societal challenges. Break down silos and encourage cross-departmental collaboration to maximize the agency's collective impact.

Community Engagement:

Engage with the community to understand its needs and involve stakeholders in the decision-making process. Building relationships with the community reinforces the agency's commitment to public service.

Innovation and Adaptive Thinking:
Encourage a culture of innovation and adaptive thinking. Given the evolving nature of societal challenges, agencies must be open to new ideas and approaches that can lead to more effective solutions.

Empower Employees to Drive Change:

Empower employees to be agents of positive change. Encourage them to propose and implement initiatives that improve processes, enhance service delivery, and align with the agency's mission.

Measure Impact and Accountability:

Establish clear metrics to measure the impact of the agency's programs and services. Emphasize accountability and data-driven decision-making to ensure the agency is fulfilling its mission effectively.

Cultivating a winning culture in government and non-profit agencies is paramount for achieving meaningful societal impact. By focusing on clear values, leadership commitment, transparent communication, and employee empowerment, these organizations can create environments that attract top talent, inspire collaboration, and drive innovation. A strong organizational culture not only enhances employee satisfaction and engagement but also contributes to the agency's ability to address complex challenges and serve the public effectively. In the realm of public service, a winning culture is the cornerstone of lasting impact and success.

6

Be The Change

"We but mirror the world. All the tendencies present in the outer world are to be found in the world of our body. If we could change ourselves, the tendencies in the world would also change. As a man changes his own nature, so does the attitude of the world change towards him. This is the divine mystery supreme. A wonderful thing it is and the source of our happiness. We need not wait to see what others do." – Mahatma Gandhi

Here is the secret, and this may be hard for you to hear. Everything starts with you. If you call off, your staff sees this, and they will call off. If you show up late, your staff will show up late. My days off were Sunday and Monday, but I had a staff member that would call off on Mondays. Now, keep in mind, I did NOT call off, but because my clinic staff worked Monday through Friday, and I was off on Monday, they would call off on Monday because I was not there to hold them accountable. I still held them accountable, but in their mind, at least they did not disappoint me when I was working. I have had staff tell me they feared disappointing me. That just blew me away. I could understand not wanting to disappoint your parents or family, but I'm just a supervisor. However, if you lead, and set an example, your staff will respect your work ethic and care about what you think of them.

I will admit that I have had some amazing supervisors that inspired my leadership style. Before I became a supervisor, I referred to this as the "Bell Curve of Supervisor Usefulness"

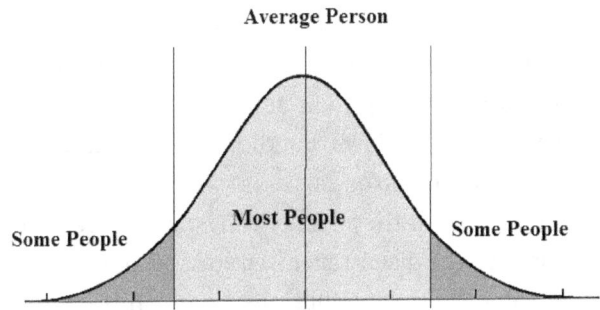

When you want help, you want someone on the far right of the bell curve, and those are the supervisors that we dump on because they will do their very best to meet your needs. We love them, but we also wear them out. In a pinch, we will lean into the people in the average section and hope to bring them towards the upper strata, with mixed results. We have zero use for the people on the left side of the curve. However, use caution with this seemingly useless group of people, especially if they are supervisors, because clearly they are politically savvy and you can learn a lot from how they manage to move forward without seeming to know anything. Never burn bridges, even if you know how to swim.

Lead by example

Demonstrate the values that you wish to see in others. When you demonstrate good attendance, punctuality, collaboration, and a commitment to excellence that sets the tone for the team. Focus on your team. Establish expectations and meet them. Raise the bar.

Establish goals and clear the path of obstacles to the goal

Goals get set forth, often by upper management. Get buy-in from your staff by asking their advice on how to meet the objectives. The goal is top-down, but the solution really needs to be ground-up. I never fail to be amazed at what staff accomplish when you ask them what they think the best way to get it done is. All of the sudden the disenfranchised staff becomes engaged because you value their contributions. That shift can move mountains for staff that have mastery of their job, but do not feel appreciated for what they do. As supervisors we can clear obstacles to achieving our overall goals.

Initiate positive changes and be solution-oriented

It is easy to find fault in anything, but can you actually offer a solution? Identifying problems is helpful, but solutions create positive change. Challenge your staff and yourself to go beyond the criticism. "Negative Nellies" can sabotage change and growth without ever stretching into ideas. It takes courage to offer ideas, be open to the innovation that can come from the front line staff with "boots on the ground". Never lose sight of the fact that these are the experts of how things are going down at the front. When everything is going well, they make us look amazing. When things go "off the rails," metrics will completely tank. If we are resilient and open to ideas, we can get back on track. Learning from our mistakes, and getting better because we learned how to NOT do it. Also keep in mind, the more solutions to the problems you get from front line staff, the more likely they are to buy into the goals and process.

Celebrate achievements

We often get bogged down with everything that is wrong, that is why it is important to recognize the contributions and achievements in a real way. Staff do not want platitudes, they want specifics. That "inspirational" email that goes out to all staff misses the mark with the staff that are actually doing the work and working hard, because the person next to them that does not perform half as well as they do gets the exact same email. Take the time to find the good work and recognize each individual's accomplishments and grow them toward the collaborative team. Never forget to say "Thank you."

Take responsibility

Like it or not, the buck stops with you. If your staff fails, you fail. Think about that for a moment. If you are feeling a bit uneasy or nauseous, that is understandable. I understand that you do not work every day, and that your staff have to be accountable for their actions as well. However, pointing fingers outward is not a good look. When you delegate a task, you have to make sure that the person you are delegating the task to has all the tools they need to get the job done. Working with staff one on one, coaching them, making sure they understand all of the expectations of the role and the responsibilities that go along with it can be a game changer.

Being the change in your organization is not a grand gesture but a series of intentional, positive actions. By embodying the values and behaviors you wish to see, fostering collaboration, and initiating improvements, you become a driving force for positive transformation. Remember that positive change often starts at the individual level, and collectively, these individual efforts can shape a culture of excellence, innovation, and collaboration within the organization. As you strive to be the change, you contribute to creating a workplace that thrives on continuous improvement and shared success.

7

The Inner Boss

There is this funny meme that says, it is hard to soar like an eagle when you are surrounded by turkeys.

I understand that you may feel pulled down by your team, your peers, your supervisors and managers, or perhaps even the work that you do. Sometimes we may not feel passionate about the work we are doing, or the reasons we are doing it. When you work in corrections, as an example, the general public views you differently. When I tell people I worked at Disneyland (which I did) there are smiles and they want to know more details. Even when I tell them I worked in Custodial, they are enthusiastic. Nobody really wants details of what it is like to be a prison nurse. I remember once while cleaning a restroom a mom said to her daughter, "This is why you study in school, so you don't end up like her." Oh the irony. There is a part of me that would love to tell her, "Hey lady, I studied so much that I ended up in prison." I loved working at Disneyland, I loved being a custodian. The key is embracing what you are doing, no matter what that is, and doing your very best. That is the Inner Boss.

During a speech in October 1967. Dr. Martin Luther King, Jr. posed the question, "What is your life's blueprint?" The bottom line is about excellence.

"If it falls your lot to be a street sweeper, sweep streets like Michelangelo painted pictures, sweep streets like Beethoven composed music, sweep streets like Leontyne Price sings before the Metropolitan Opera. Sweep streets like Shakespeare wrote poetry. Sweep streets so well that all the hosts of heaven and earth will have to pause and say: Here lived a great street sweeper who swept his job well." - Dr. Martin Luther King, Jr.

It is easy to look at other people and think that you should just do less because everyone else does. If that is your thinking, you are part of the problem.

There can be many obstacles to doing any job, but effort should not be one of them. Some of my peers complain of how much work they have to do, and the challenges of meeting deadlines. Well, show up for work, it is amazing how easy it is to get things done when you are present and working. Trying to do a full-time job with part-time hours would make the job much more challenging but it is completely avoidable. People get sick, accidents happen, but when they occur just on Fridays and Mondays it seems a bit suspect.

The Inner Boss is about accountability to yourself, but can also manifest as your accountability to others. There can be obstacles to accountability, these are also referred to as "excuses" If we understand the "excuses" and what drives them, we can overcome them.

Common excuses people make:

1. Lack of Time:

Excuse: "I didn't have enough time to complete the task."

- *Addressing the Issue:* Time management skills are essential. Encourage individuals to prioritize tasks, set realistic deadlines, and avoid procrastination.

2. Insufficient Resources:

Excuse: "I couldn't do a good job because I didn't have the necessary resources."

- *Addressing the Issue:* Encourage proactive resource management. Individuals should communicate resource needs in advance and explore alternative solutions.

3. Blaming Others:

Excuse: "It's not my fault; someone else didn't do their part."

- *Addressing the Issue:* Promote a culture of accountability. Encourage individuals to focus on their responsibilities and collaborate with team members to address challenges.

4. Perfectionism:

Excuse: "I couldn't finish the task because I wanted it to be perfect."

- *Addressing the Issue:* Emphasize the importance of completion over perfection. Encourage individuals to set realistic standards and iterate on their work.

5. Lack of Skills or Training:

Excuse: "I couldn't do a good job because I don't have the necessary skills."

- *Addressing the Issue:* Identify skill gaps and provide training opportunities. Encourage a growth mindset and a willingness to learn.

6. Fear of Failure:

Excuse: "I was afraid of failing, so I didn't give it my best effort."

- *Addressing the Issue:* Foster a culture that embraces failure as a part of the learning process. Encourage individuals to take calculated risks and learn from mistakes.

7. Overwhelmed by Priorities:

Excuse: "I had too many tasks, and I couldn't focus on doing a good job."

- *Addressing the Issue:* Help individuals prioritize tasks and set realistic expectations. Encourage effective time management and delegation when needed.

8. Lack of Motivation:

Excuse: "I didn't feel motivated, so I didn't put in my best effort."

- *Addressing the Issue:* Explore the root cause of motivation issues. Encourage individuals to find intrinsic motivation, set personal goals, and connect their work to a larger purpose.

9. Communication Breakdown:

Excuse: "I didn't know what was expected of me."

- *Addressing the Issue:* Improve communication channels.

Ensure that expectations are clearly communicated, and provide a platform for individuals to seek clarification.

10. Poor Planning:

Excuse: "I didn't plan my work properly, and things fell through the cracks."

- *Addressing the Issue:* Emphasize the importance of effective planning. Encourage individuals to create actionable plans, set milestones, and regularly review progress.

11. External Factors:

Excuse: "There were external factors beyond my control that affected my performance."

- *Addressing the Issue:* Acknowledge external challenges but emphasize personal responsibility and proactive problem-solving.

8

Conclusion

There you have it! All of my thoughts that a new supervisor will need to build a successful team. A new supervisor stepping into a role carries the responsibility of guiding and inspiring their team. Key traits essential for success in this role include effective communication, adaptability, and a collaborative mindset. A strong leader fosters open lines of communication, ensuring that team members feel heard and understood. Adaptability allows the leader to navigate change confidently, inspiring resilience and flexibility within the team. Collaborative leaders recognize the value of collective efforts, encouraging a team-oriented approach to problem-solving and decision-making.

Empathy is a crucial trait that enables leaders to understand and support their team members on both professional and personal levels. Visionary leadership, coupled with the ability to set clear goals, provides a sense of direction, motivating the team toward shared objectives. A commitment to continuous learning and self-improvement demonstrates humility and a dedication to personal and professional growth. Lastly, a new supervisor should exhibit strong decision-making skills, balancing assertiveness with openness to input, fostering a positive and productive work environment. By embodying these traits, a new supervisor establishes a foundation for effective leadership and team success.

I hope you found this brief book helpful as you endeavor on your path as a supervisor. If you found it helpful, I would be very appreciative of a positive review on Amazon.

9

Reading List

Recommended reading list for leadership and personal development

Brown, B. (2010). *The Gifts of Imperfection: Let Go of Who You Think You're Supposed to Be and Embrace Who You Are.* Hazelden.

Brown, B. (2018). *Dare to Lead: Brave Work. Tough Conversations. Whole Hearts.* Random House.

Cain, S. (2012). *Quiet: The Power of Introverts in a World That Can't Stop Talking.* Crown Publishers.

Clear, J. (2018). *Atomic Habits: An Easy & Proven Way to Build Good Habits & Break Bad Ones.* Avery.

Collins, J. (2001). *Good to Great: Why Some Companies Make the Leap and Others Don't.* HarperBusiness.

Covey, S. R. (1989). *The 7 Habits of Highly Effective People: Powerful Lessons in Personal Change.* Free Press.

Duckworth, A. (2016). *Grit: The Power of Passion and Perseverance.* Scribner.

Duckworth, A., Peterson, C., Matthews, M. D., & Kelly, D. R. (2007). Grit: Perseverance and passion for long-term goals. *Journal of Personality and Social Psychology, 92*(6), 1087–1101.

Dweck, C. S. (2006). *Mindset: The New Psychology of Success.* Random House.

Goleman, D. (1995). *Emotional Intelligence: Why It Can Matter More Than IQ.* Bantam Books.

Maxwell, J. C. (2007). *The 21 Irrefutable Laws of Leadership: Follow Them and People Will Follow You.* Thomas Nelson.

Pink, D. H. (2011). *Drive: The Surprising Truth About What Motivates Us.* Riverhead Books.

Willink, J., & Babin, L. (2015). *Extreme Ownership: How U.S. Navy SEALs Lead and Win.* St. Martin's Press.

www.ingramcontent.com/pod-product-compliance
Lightning Source LLC
Chambersburg PA
CBHW072223290526
45794CB00007B/2872